# SEWING

**WRITTEN BY JUDY ANN SADLER**
illustrated by Marilyn Mets

KIDS CAN PRESS LTD.
Toronto

To my parents, Frank and Rieka Bertens,
for stitching our family together with love

**Canadian Cataloguing in Publication Data**

Sadler, Judy Ann, 1959-
        Sewing

(Kids Can Easy Crafts)
ISBN 1-55074-101-2

1. Sewing – Juvenile literature.  2. Sewing.
I. Mets, Marilyn.  II. Title.  III. Series.

TT712.S23 1993   j646.2            C92-094483-3

Kids Can Press Ltd.              Edited by Laurie Wark
585½ Bloor Street West           Designed by N.R. Jackson
Toronto, Ontario, Canada         Printed and bound in Hong Kong
M6G 1K5
                                 93 0 9 8 7 6 5 4 3 2 1

# CONTENTS

# GETTING STARTED

Do you realize that many things you wear or use are sewn together? Pants, shirts, skirts, coats, curtains, pillows, towels, sheets and shoes. They're all made of fabric pieces stitched together. In this book you will see how to cut, pin and stitch many neat things. Make bows, beanbags, sock sacks, puppets and jazzed-up clothes. Create one-of-a-kind gifts for your friends and family. Sewing is fun, fast and handy. So gather the materials you see on these pages and be sure to keep the needles, pins and buttons away from your younger brother or sister. Happy sewing!

# Materials

**Needles** You'll need sharps and darners. Sharps are long and thin with a small eye (hole). Use them with regular thread. Darners are thick and have a big eye. Use them with yarn and embroidery floss. Store needles in their package or in a pin cushion.

**Thread, yarn and embroidery floss** The colour should match your fabric, unless you want the thread to stand out.

**Fabric** Felt is good because it does not fray or ravel. You'll also need other fabrics, such as cottons. Socks are good, too. Often one sock in a pair gets worn-out before the other. Use the good sock and parts of the worn-out sock to make things. If you don't have fabric around home, look in the remnant bins at fabric stores. If your fabric is wrinkled, ask an adult to help you iron it before you begin a project.

**Scissors** You'll need sharp scissors to cut fabric and thread. Handle them carefully and ask an adult for help if you need it.

**Pinking shears** These cut a zigzag edge that prevents fabrics from ravelling. If you have them, use them for cutting fabrics (except felt) or when you want to have a decorative edge. Ask an adult for help if you need it.

**Straight pins** Pins hold your fabric together in the right place while you sew. Handle them carefully and keep them in a small container or pin cushion.

**Stuffing** Use clean soft rags, clean cut-up old pantihose or polyester fibre fill.

fabric scraps + stuffing

# Helpful Hints

**Threading a needle** Cut a piece of thread so that the ends are unfrayed. Wet one end of the thread with your lips and poke it through the eye of the needle, or use a needle threader as shown.

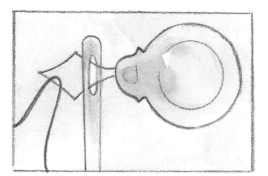

Make a knot at one end of the thread, so that it won't pull through the fabric. Always tuck the knot where it will not show.

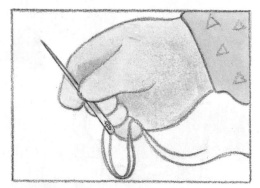

**Holding the needle** Hold the needle between your thumb and index finger and use your middle finger to help push the needle through the fabric (you might want to wear a thimble on your middle finger). As you sew, hold on to the thread with your baby finger, or it will pull out of the needle.

## SEWING ON BUTTONS

1. Double the thread by making both strands the same length and knotting them together at the end.

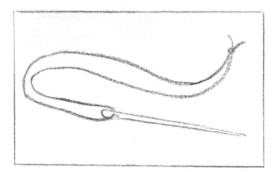

2. Poke the needle up from under the fabric where the button will go. Place the button on the needle.

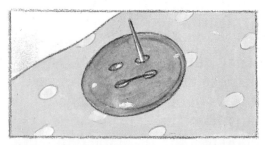

3. Go down through the hole beside the one your needle came up in. Sew each pair of holes about five times.

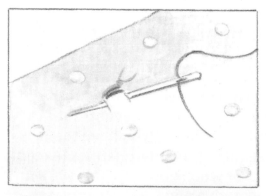

4. Before cutting the thread, make a couple of small stitches at the back of the fabric.

# Basic Stitches

## RUNNING STITCH

1. Bring the needle up through the fabric.

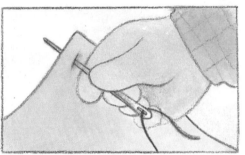

2. Poke the needle back down through the fabric beside where your needle came up. Keep bringing the needle up and back down. Make the spaces and stitches even and not too tight.

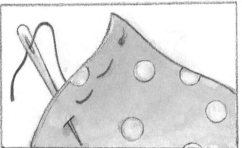

3. To finish off, stitch on top of the last stitch two times before you cut the thread.

## OVERCAST STITCH

1. Bring the needle up through the fabric.

2. Bring the needle over the top of the fabric and poke it into the back near the first stitch. Pull the needle through to the front.

3. Keep the stitches even. To finish off, make a couple of stitches on top of the last one and cut the thread.

## BACKSTITCH

1. Bring the needle up through the fabric and back down close to the first stitch. Come up through the fabric again as you would for the running stitch.

2. Poke the tip of the needle into the fabric at the end of the first stitch. Bring the needle out again in front of the thread and pull it through.

3. Keep the stitches even. To finish off, sew a couple of stitches on top of the last one and cut the thread.

# FELT BAG

**THINGS YOU NEED:**

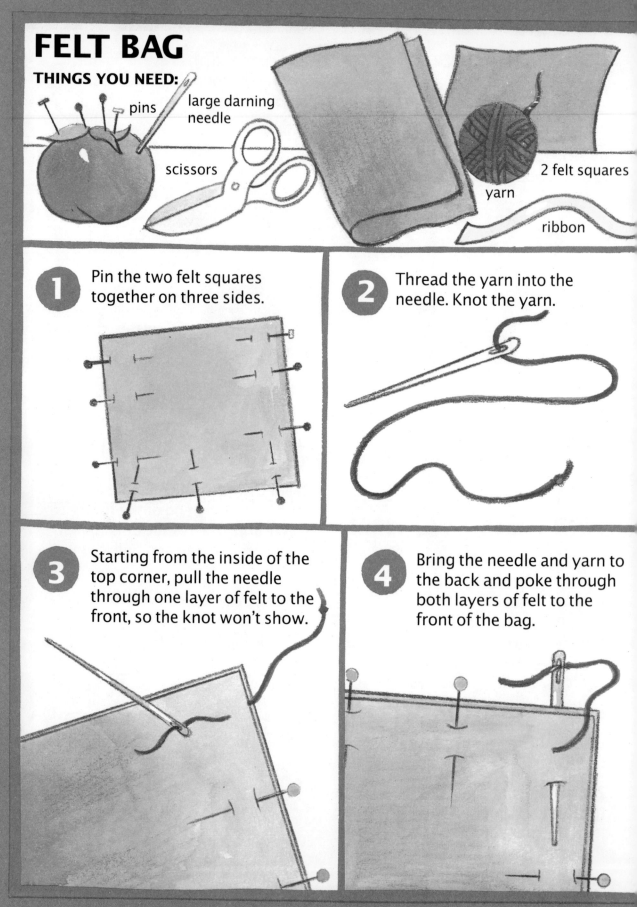

pins

large darning needle

scissors

yarn

2 felt squares

ribbon

**1** Pin the two felt squares together on three sides.

**2** Thread the yarn into the needle. Knot the yarn.

**3** Starting from the inside of the top corner, pull the needle through one layer of felt to the front, so the knot won't show.

**4** Bring the needle and yarn to the back and poke through both layers of felt to the front of the bag.

**5** Use the running stitch to sew around the three sides. Remove the pins as you sew.

**6** When you reach the end, make a few extra stitches on top of the last one and poke the needle through one layer to the inside of the bag. Knot the yarn and cut it.

**7** Fold down the top of the bag about 5 cm (2 inches). Make four evenly spaced cuts through both layers along this folded edge. Unfold.

**8** Starting at the centre of the bag, weave the ribbon through the slits. Be sure to leave enough ribbon on each end to tie the bag closed.

# Fun ideas to try

♥ Use two different colours of felt for your bag.

♥ Make a bag out of regular fabric. Use pinking shears to cut out your squares.

# SOCK SACK

**THINGS YOU NEED:**

darning needle

old sock

yarn

scissors

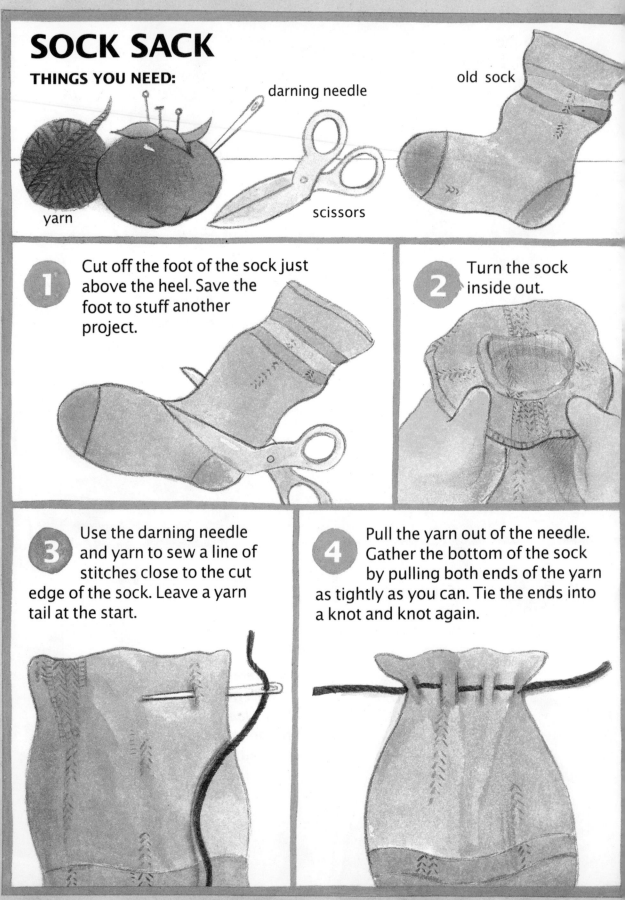

**1** Cut off the foot of the sock just above the heel. Save the foot to stuff another project.

**2** Turn the sock inside out.

**3** Use the darning needle and yarn to sew a line of stitches close to the cut edge of the sock. Leave a yarn tail at the start.

**4** Pull the yarn out of the needle. Gather the bottom of the sock by pulling both ends of the yarn as tightly as you can. Tie the ends into a knot and knot again.

**5** Turn the sock right side out. To make the drawstrings, loosely sew a row of running stitches around the top of the sock. Leave a yarn tail.

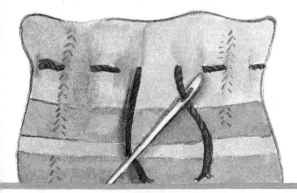

**6** Pull the yarn out of the needle and knot the ends together.

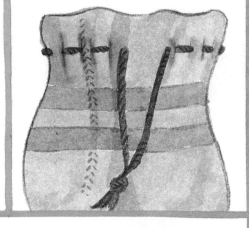

**7** Now start at the opposite side and run another row of stitches just below the first row. Be careful not to catch your first row of stitches with the needle. Knot the ends together.

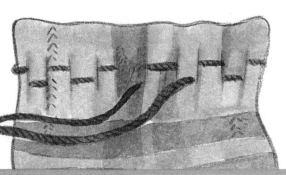

**8** Hold one drawstring in each hand and pull in opposite directions. Now you have a handy sack for marbles, stones, a small gift or some other treasure.

# Fun ideas to try

☺ Use brightly coloured yarn for the drawstrings.

☺ Make a larger bag by using an old pair of track pants cut off just below the knee.

# BEANBAG

**THINGS YOU NEED:**

pins

needle

scissors

thread

fabric

dried beans (such as kidney or white navy)

**1** Cut out a rectangle of fabric twice as big as you want your beanbag to be.

**2** Fold the rectangle in half with the good sides together. Pin it on three sides, but leave an opening.

**3** Use the backstitch to sew it together. Make small stitches so that the beans cannot fall out. Remove the pins as you sew.

**4** Whenever your thread becomes too short, make a couple of tiny stitches on top of the last stitch so that the other stitches do not come loose. Remember to knot your new piece of thread.

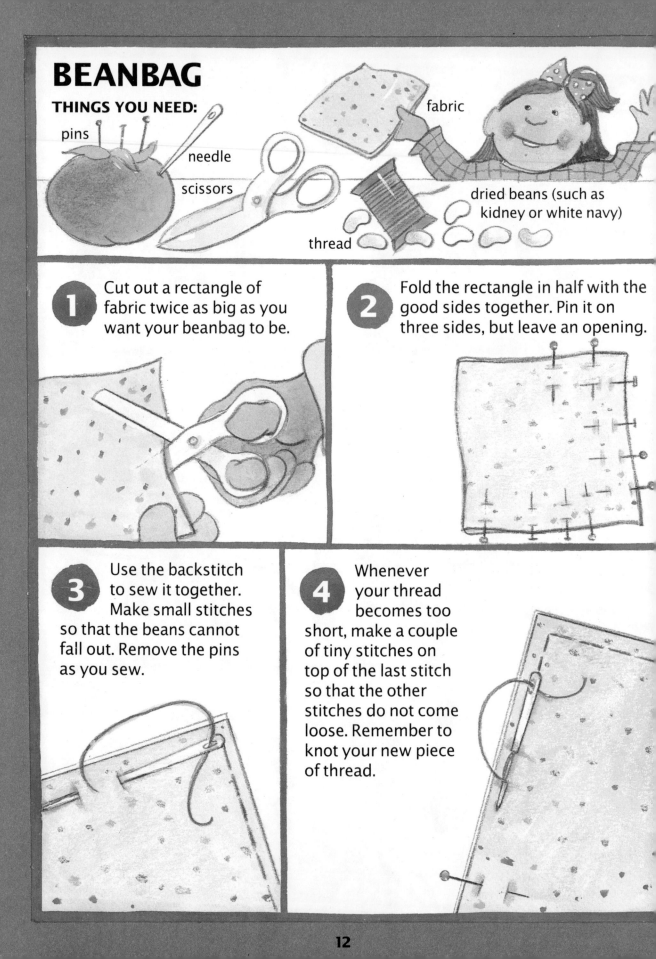

**5** Turn the beanbag right side out. Gently poke the corners out with a closed pair of scissors.

**6** Fill the bag with beans so that it is plump but not tight.

**7** Tuck in the unfinished edges and stitch the beanbag closed.

**8** Have a beanbag toss with your friends. Place three different-sized boxes on the floor. The large box is worth 5 points, the medium box is worth 10 points, and the small box is worth 20 points. Whoever has the most points after five tosses wins.

## Fun ideas to try

Instead of filling the bag with beans, stuff it to make a pin cushion.

# PLACEMATS

**THINGS YOU NEED:**

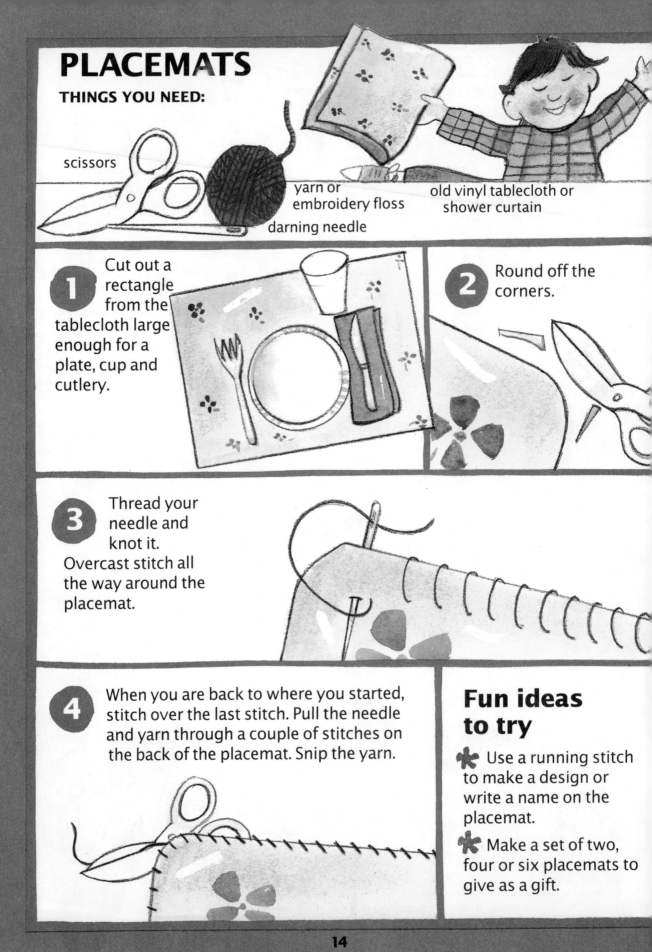

scissors

yarn or
embroidery floss

darning needle

old vinyl tablecloth or
shower curtain

**1** Cut out a rectangle from the tablecloth large enough for a plate, cup and cutlery.

**2** Round off the corners.

**3** Thread your needle and knot it. Overcast stitch all the way around the placemat.

**4** When you are back to where you started, stitch over the last stitch. Pull the needle and yarn through a couple of stitches on the back of the placemat. Snip the yarn.

## Fun ideas to try

✳ Use a running stitch to make a design or write a name on the placemat.

✳ Make a set of two, four or six placemats to give as a gift.

# SERVIETTES

**THINGS YOU NEED:**

thread

pinking shears

needle

washable fabric

**1** Cut out large squares of fabric with the pinking shears.

**2** Ask an adult to help you fold down and iron the edges all around your serviette. Start at the top, then do the bottom and then press the sides. The corners will overlap. (If you did not cut with pinking shears, double fold and press each side so that the unfinished edges do not show.)

**3** Use small running stitches to hem the edges of your serviette. Hide the knot under a pressed edge.

## Fun ideas to try

★ Use a colour of thread that will stand out.

★ Stitch your initials into a corner.

★ Make a set of serviettes to give as a gift with the placemats you made.

# PENCIL CASE

**THINGS YOU NEED:**

pins

darning needle

yarn

felt

scissors

ruler or measuring tape

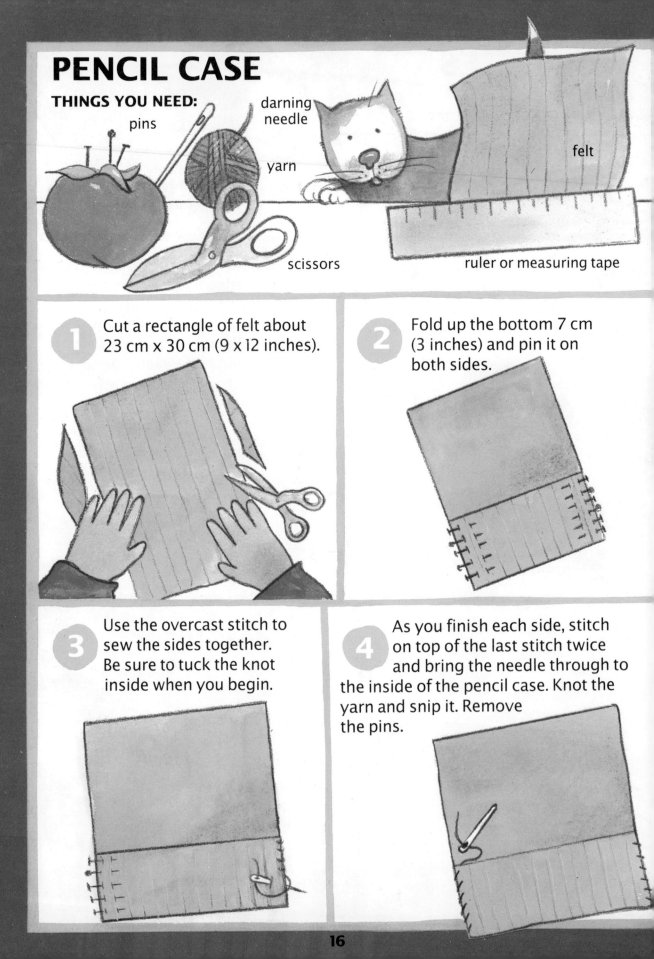

**1** Cut a rectangle of felt about 23 cm x 30 cm (9 x 12 inches).

**2** Fold up the bottom 7 cm (3 inches) and pin it on both sides.

**3** Use the overcast stitch to sew the sides together. Be sure to tuck the knot inside when you begin.

**4** As you finish each side, stitch on top of the last stitch twice and bring the needle through to the inside of the pencil case. Knot the yarn and snip it. Remove the pins.

**5** Round off the top two corners.

**6** Flip the pencil case over. Poke the darning needle and yarn down through the centre of the flap and then pull them back up.

**7** Take the yarn out of the needle. Tie the two ends into a knot to hold the yarn in place. Make a knot at each end.

**8** To close the pencil case, roll it up from the bottom and tie the yarn around it in a bow.

## Fun ideas to try

✻ Make a middle-size pouch to hold jewellery, crayons or a deck of cards.

✱ Make a toothfairy pouch small enough to hold a tooth and big enough to hold coins!

# T-SHIRT PILLOW

**THINGS YOU NEED:**

scissors

needle

stuffing

old T-shirt

thread or embroidery floss

**1** Use the overcast stitch to close the neck and sleeves of your T-shirt.

**2** Put stuffing in the sleeves, around the neck and in the rest of the T-shirt so that it is plump.

**3** Use the overcast stitch to close the bottom.

## Fun ideas to try

⭐ Make a bunch of pillows for your bed, reading corner or T.V. room.

# BANDANNA NECKROLL

**THINGS YOU NEED:**

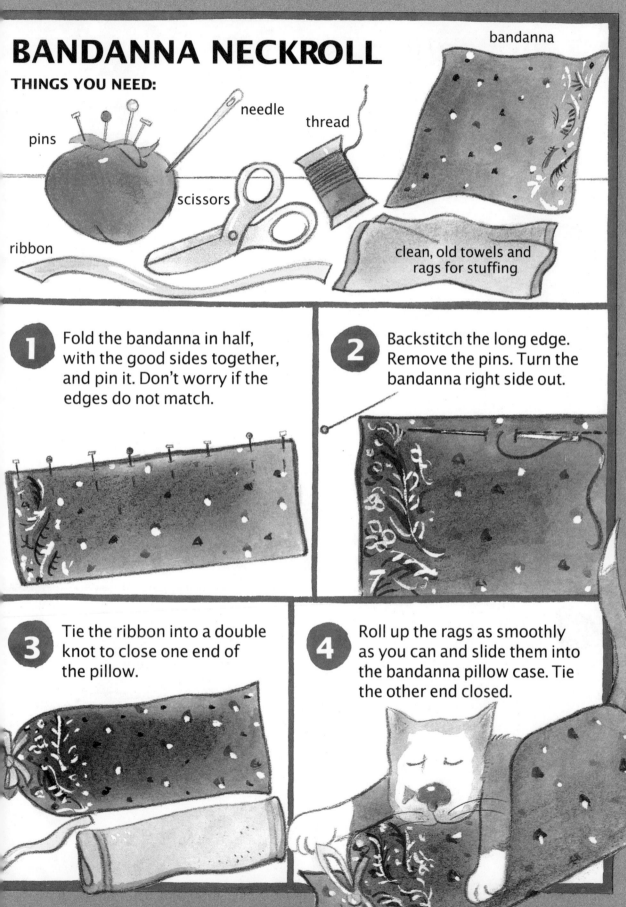

needle

thread

bandanna

pins

scissors

ribbon

clean, old towels and rags for stuffing

**1** Fold the bandanna in half, with the good sides together, and pin it. Don't worry if the edges do not match.

**2** Backstitch the long edge. Remove the pins. Turn the bandanna right side out.

**3** Tie the ribbon into a double knot to close one end of the pillow.

**4** Roll up the rags as smoothly as you can and slide them into the bandanna pillow case. Tie the other end closed.

# HAIR SCRUNCHEE

**THINGS YOU NEED:**

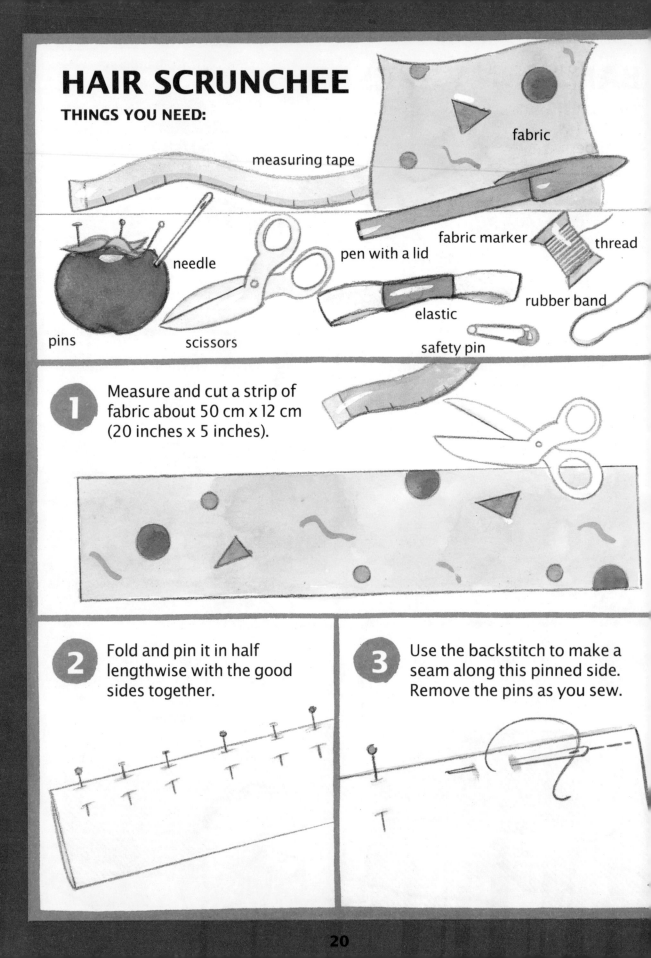

fabric

measuring tape

fabric marker

thread

pen with a lid

needle

rubber band

elastic

pins

scissors

safety pin

**1** Measure and cut a strip of fabric about 50 cm x 12 cm (20 inches x 5 inches).

**2** Fold and pin it in half lengthwise with the good sides together.

**3** Use the backstitch to make a seam along this pinned side. Remove the pins as you sew.

**4** To turn this tube right side out, place a pen in one end. Use the rubber band to hold the fabric around the pen. Push the pen down the tube, pull it out the other end and remove the rubber band.

**5** Cut a length of 6-mm (1/4-inch) wide elastic about 35 cm (14 inches) long. Attach the safety pin to one end of the elastic and use it to work the elastic down the tube of fabric.

**6** Overlap the ends of the elastic and use the overcast stitch to sew them together.

**7** Tuck one end of the tube into the other and try to match the seam. Fold under the unfinished edge of the fabric on top.

**8** Stitch the folded edge to the tucked-in edge, all the way around.

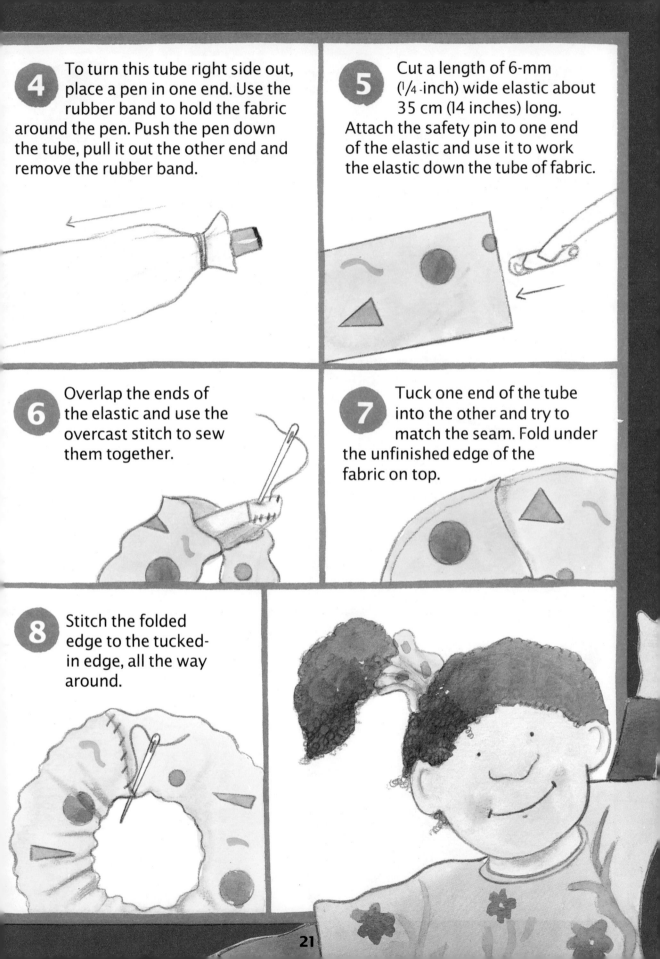

# BOW

**THINGS YOU NEED:**

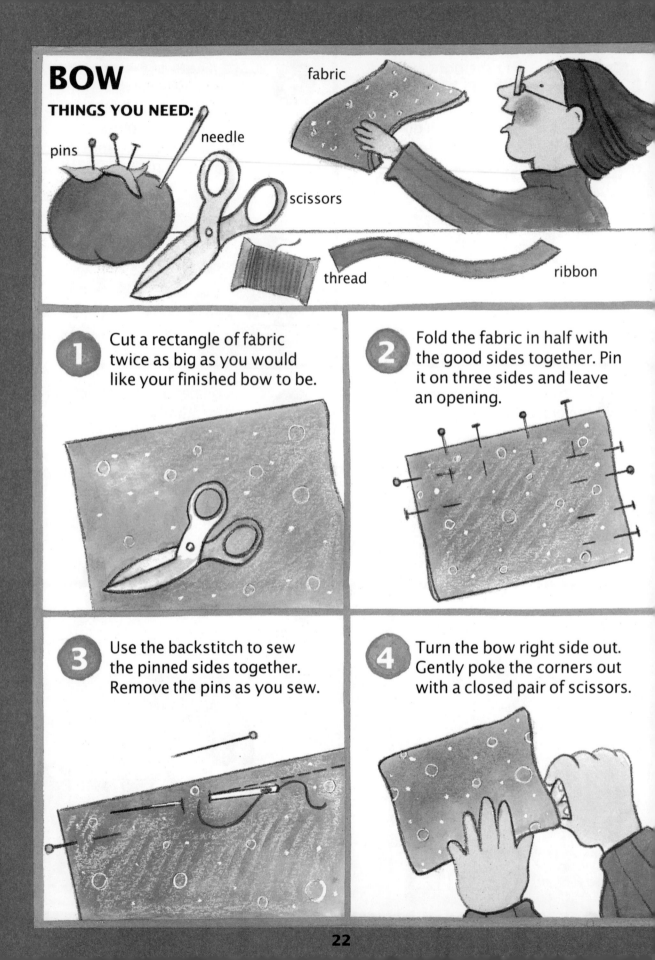

pins

needle

scissors

thread

ribbon

fabric

**1** Cut a rectangle of fabric twice as big as you would like your finished bow to be.

**2** Fold the fabric in half with the good sides together. Pin it on three sides and leave an opening.

**3** Use the backstitch to sew the pinned sides together. Remove the pins as you sew.

**4** Turn the bow right side out. Gently poke the corners out with a closed pair of scissors.

**5** Tuck the edges of the unfinished opening inside. Ask an adult to help you iron the bow flat.

**6** Stitch the opening closed as shown.

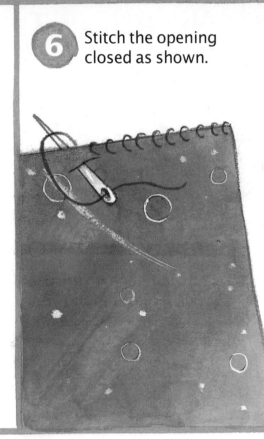

**7** Fanfold the bow. Ask someone to hold it as you tie a ribbon around the centre. Trim the ends of the ribbon.

## Fun ideas to try

 Make a giant bow for a clown costume. Use a long piece of ribbon to tie the centre of the bow and leave the ends to tie loosely around your neck.

Sew, glue or tie the bow onto a barrette, hair band or hair elastic, or slip it onto a bobby pin.

# HAND PUPPET

**THINGS YOU NEED:** darning needle

buttons and other materials for face

felt

paper

pins

yarn

scissors

pencil

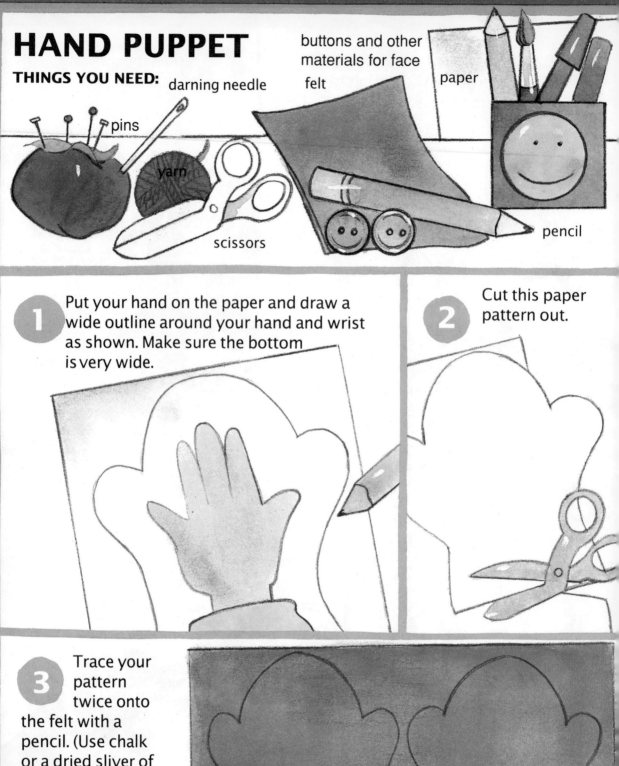

**1** Put your hand on the paper and draw a wide outline around your hand and wrist as shown. Make sure the bottom is very wide.

**2** Cut this paper pattern out.

**3** Trace your pattern twice onto the felt with a pencil. (Use chalk or a dried sliver of soap if your felt is a dark colour.)

**4** Cut out the two felt shapes.

**5** Sew on button eyes and stitch the rest of the face. If you decide to glue on the face, you can do it at the end.

**6** Pin the two felt shapes together. If your puppet needs ears, cut them out and pin them in between the two layers of felt.

**7** Use the running stitch to sew the puppet together. Remove the pins as you sew. Leave the bottom open.

## Fun ideas to try

🎀 Sew or glue on paws, a bowtie, hair, clothing, roly eyes, whiskers or a hat.

🎀 Make your hand puppet out of fabric. Use pinking shears to cut it out.

🎀 Make a lot of puppets so that you can put on a show.

# SOCK DOLL

beads, felt, yarn or fabric paint for face

**THINGS YOU NEED:**

stuffing

old sock

darning needle

yarn

needle

thread

scissors

**1** Cut off the foot part of the sock just above the heel. Put it aside. Turn the other part of the sock inside out.

**2** Use the darning needle and yarn to sew a row of running stitches close to the cut edge of the sock. Leave a yarn tail at the start.

**3** Take the yarn out of the needle. Pull both ends of the yarn tightly and knot them twice.

**4** Turn the sock right side out and stuff it.

**5** With the needle and thread use the overcast stitch to sew the open end of the sock closed. Stitch on top of the last stitch a couple of times before you snip the thread, so that the stitches do not come loose.

**6** Tie a piece of yarn below the gathered end of the sock to make your doll's head.

**7** Poke the darning needle from the back of the doll to the front. Leave a tail of yarn at the back. Now poke the needle through to the back from the front. Tie the yarn at the back. This gives your doll a waist and arms.

**8** Cut the heel off the foot part of the sock. Roll up the toe part to make a hat. Use fabric paint, felt pieces, beads or yarn to make your doll's face.

## Fun ideas to try

Braid some yarn and stitch it across your doll's head for hair.

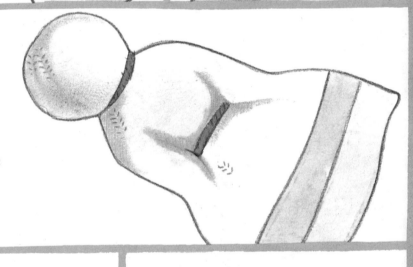

# HOBBY-HORSE

**THINGS YOU NEED:**

hockey-stick shaft, broomstick or wooden dowel

stuffing

scraps of felt

scissors

yarn

needle

darning needle

thread

2 buttons

an adult-size sock

2 thumbtacks

**1** Tightly stuff the foot of the sock. Put the stick in the sock and stuff all around it.

**2** Ask an adult to help you push tacks through the sock and into the stick. Tightly wind yarn over the tacks, around the bottom of the sock and tie it.

**3** Cut out two felt circles for eyes. Sew a button onto each one.

**4** Stitch the eyes onto the horse's head. Make a couple of tiny stitches as you finish so that the other stitches don't come loose.

**5** Cut out two felt triangles, with rounded sides, for ears. Fold each ear in half and stitch one onto each side of the sock.

**6** Cut out two more felt circles for the nostrils. Sew or glue one onto each side of your horse's muzzle.

**7** Use yarn and a darning needle to make a mane. Poke the needle in and bring it back out close by. Pull the yarn through and snip it, leaving yarn ends on both sides. Tie the ends together.

**8** Continue cutting and tying until the mane is all the way down the horse's neck.

## Fun ideas to try

Use ribbon, heavy yarn or shoelaces to make reins for your hobby-horse.

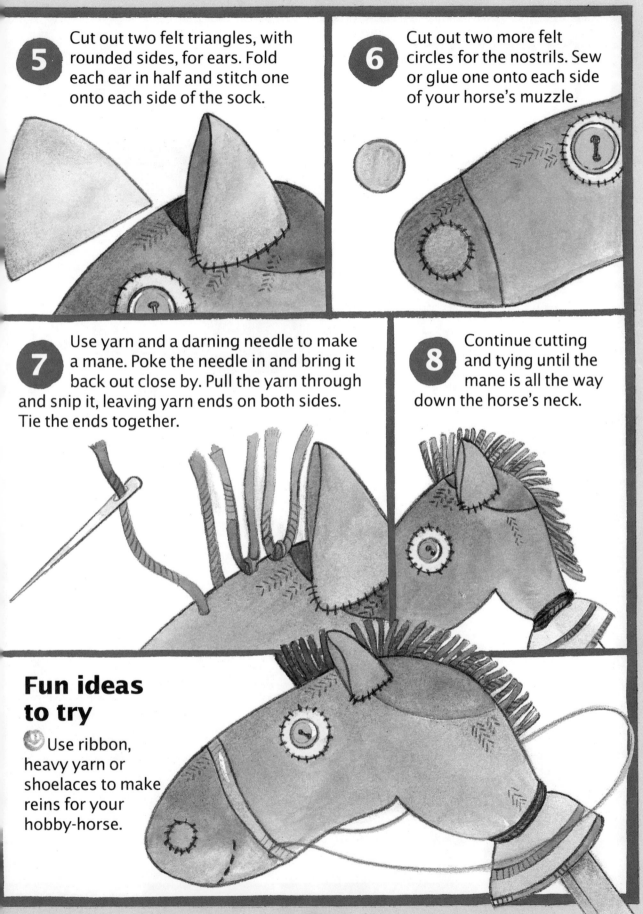

# DECORATED CLOTHING

**Shoes:** Sew all shapes and sizes of buttons onto your running shoes. Try using brightly coloured thread. Make sure the thread knot is on the inside. Be careful not to poke your fingers. Sew jingling bells on the toes of your shoes.

**T-shirts:** Use the running stitch to outline stars, hearts, flowers or your initials. Sew on rows of buttons and beads. Create stripes of colour by sewing on ribbon, rickrack and other trims. Sew on sequins, lace, glittering buttons and bows. You can also jazz up jackets, jeans and shorts with these same ideas.

**Mittens and Gloves:** Try sewing on button eyes, felt ears, a felt tongue and yarn hair to make mitten puppets. The fingers on gloves can become fairy tale characters. Use yarn, felt, buttons and fabric paint to create Goldilocks and the Three Bears or the gang from The Wizard of Oz.

**Hats:** Make a hat that is specially decorated for a friend, family member or yourself. For someone who likes to go fishing, sew on felt fish, sinkers, bobbers, rubber worms and other fishing tackle (without hooks). For a nature lover, sew on silk or dried flowers, pom-pom caterpillars, twigs and feathers. Other ideas are: badges, bells, beads, bows, buttons, rickrack, ribbon, keys, keychains, plastic animals, tiny dolls, doll accessories and other toys and trinkets.

# AND SEW ON ...
## Here are more ideas to keep you sewing!

**Cookie-cutter Shapes:** Trace a cookie-cutter shape twice onto felt. Cut the shapes out and pin them together. Just before you finish stitching all around the felt, stuff the shape a little bit. Finish the stitching. Pin it to your hat or T-shirt. Or fasten a string to it and hang it on a doorknob, Christmas tree or around your neck.

**Felt Cube:** Use a paper pattern to cut out six felt squares. Use the overcast stitch to join four of them together. (This will take four seams.) Stitch the fifth square on all four sides to the bottom. Now stitch down two sides on the top, stuff the cube and finish by sewing the other two seams. Be sure to tuck all the knots and finishing threads to the inside of the cube as you go. If you make another cube and glue felt dots on all six sides of each, you'll have a set of dice!

**Worm:** Cut a long strip of fabric. Fold and pin it with good sides together. Trim one end so that it is rounded. Begin backstitching the rounded end and continue down the long edge. Leave the other end open. Use a knitting needle or long-handled spoon to turn the fabric right side out. Stuff it. Sew the end closed. The rounded end is the worm's head. Sew on buttons or felt for eyes.